VOCATION

VOCATION

T R Glover

BEAUCHIEF
ABBEY·PRESS

Published by Beauchief Abbey Press, June 2021

www.beauchiefabbeypress.org.uk

ISBN 978-1-9164021-9-5

A CIP catalogue record for this title is available from the British Library.

Cover design by Michael Lindley, Truth Studio, Sheffield
www.truthstudio.co.uk

CONTENTS

FOREWORD

Just before setting off for St Stephen's House in 1985 to begin my ordination training, my Dad gave me a book of prayers, and writing on the inside cover he expressed his deep desire that I should 'flourish in my chosen vocation'. Seeing his words my Mum noted the contradiction of the words 'chosen vocation'; by its very nature vocation is a call, not a choice. T R Glover would have nodded in approval.

The Bible tells of a divine call to Isaiah in the Temple amidst smoke, cherubim, burning coals and the awesome presence of God, and Isaiah responds with words that resound in the heart of anyone discerning the call of God in this or any age, 'Here am I, send me!' The call was from the throne of grace and majesty, and yet the voice that responded was of Isaiah's frail flesh. I have no doubt that any ordination selection process would look dimly on anyone so cocky as to step forward and invoke the Lord of Heaven and earth to 'bring it on!', so I would like to think that Isaiah's voice quivered as he uttered those words. Either way, the prophet's commission was both a call, a response and, dare I say, a decision.

The New Testament presents us with the call of the disciples, where the simple words 'Follow me' have an urgency and an explicit offer. Matthew is called out of his tax collecting booth; Peter, James and John fished for a living. Both Isaiah and the fishermen could have turned their heads in a moment and carried on with their lives; such is the precarious nature of vocation. There is a definite decision to embark on the journey - both to be sent and to follow. From the start God equips the situation. In Isaiah's case an angel with a burning coal anoints the prophet's lips to bestow on him the eloquence that his response to God's call requires. Meanwhile, the account of the fishermen's calling is set alongside a great haul of fish, which leaves the family of James and John well provided for and space cleared for the brothers to discern what 'Follow me!' might mean.

Some who come to know the offer and call of God and the church describe the journey as God's relentless pursuit of them over many years and this sometimes sounds as though responding to God's call is something that happens once they are finally ground down. Yet vocation can also be testimony not only to the persistence of God but to the power of 'Yes!'

This new edition of Glover's powerful exploration of vocation from 1913 is issued to mark the forming of a partnership. St Illtud's Church in Llantwit Major in South Wales holds the legacy of Illtud, who established a seat of Christian learning on the site in the sixth century. Fifteen centuries later, the same tradition is being recovered and proclaimed in territory that is familiar to Coleridge in Wales, a creative organisation that will help this new partnership explore relational Christian traditions, some of which shaped the 'broad church' movement of the mid nineteenth century which Glover develops. The partnership seeks to give a relevant voice to both traditions as they meet, interact and inform the search for the Kingdom of Heaven in everyday life, much as Glover did a century ago. In practical terms, this is marked by a library and well-visited sacred spaces that speak today of God's presence in prayer and worship, reflection and practice, with signposts that are much deeper, marking a journey that has travelled from the mists of Celtic times, and which continues today.

The establishment of the Kingdom of Heaven Library at 'Llanilltud' is a testament to the power of 'Yes!', when God's purposes are seen through the prism of scholarship, personal faith and a commitment to offer welcome that is without condition. It reveals a deep desire to allow faith, history, heritage and culture to be companions on a road that is lit by the light of Christ and which journeys towards the Kingdom of God.

This project has only emerged because those involved believe in the power of 'Yes!'; it is of Christ, it is a new creation and, in its life, work and witness, it allows the Kingdom of God to shed its light on all those drawn to it, so that all may see life afresh and anew. In countless ways, that is vocation.

Edwin Counsell
Llantwit Major, 2021

INTRODUCTION

This book is published to celebrate the opening of a new venture called The Library at Llantwit. The Library project is a cultural exploration undertaken between the congregation at St Illtud's church in Llantwit Major and the cultural facilitation company Coleridge in Wales Ltd to celebrate the offer of the remarkable intellectual and cultural Christian heritage in the historic town of Llantwit Major, South Wales.

Choosing this text by T R Glover sets a challenge to book and literature detectives: can you obtain a copy of the original? It appears as a missing text. T R Glover became a leading British scholar of his day on the history and literature of ancient Greece and Rome and for many years was Public Orator of Cambridge University. His active life supporting the Baptist church led him to become well known for his books on Jesus and the early church on which he brought to bear his considerable intellectual and cultural gifts. He is probably best known today for his book *The Jesus of History*.[1]

This book, Glover's *Vocation*, was published as a booklet for the Student Christian Movement in 1913 and today copies of the pamphlet are almost impossible to come across, even through online library catalogues. I chanced across a single securely bound edition one day in a secondhand book market. It immediately struck me as a text about the motive force of Christianity. Glover's voice is fresh and confident. He seeks to skip past ecclesiastical concern, cultural anxieties and institutional blockages and present the personal call of Jesus directly to us that we might explore the biggest questions of life and relationship.

Glover's writing is both very old and quite new. Its age comes from its fabulous pedigree of Christian scholarship and Christian witness. Glover is expert in the literature of the declining Roman Empire and knows the history and writings of the early church. In this book he handles old texts with skill and great personal sensitivity, illuminating discoveries made by the friends and acquaintances of Jesus. This book is new, or

---

[1] Modern edition with introduction by J W Rogerson published in 2017 by Beauchief Abbey Press

fresh, in that it remains relevant today. There was a great 19th century movement in England whose work is celebrated with these inspiring words,

> Where else in the history of human thought is there a more remarkable combination of Christian idealism with love of truth, devotion to liberty, and yearning for intellectual and social unity? Where else is to be found a more vigorous body of ideas and experience relative to these?[2]

and Glover's work belongs directly to these traditions. It is these wonderful, open, social, aesthetic and intellectual traditions, and their Welsh counterparts, that the Library at Llantwit seeks and serves today. They are the remarkable relational Christian traditions. There is a great contemporary need in British culture for discovery that the Christian tradtion is a free, energetic, creative, intellectually enquiring and robust adventure that engages with our whole personal and communal life. Glover celebrated and championed this, and the Library at Llantwit seeks to do the same.

Additionally, this book is a particularly good choice for the opening of the Library at Llantwit because in the final chapter Glover relates a short story in which a sculptor living in a

---

2 C R Sanders, *Coleridge and the Broad Church Movement*, Duke University Press, 1942

small town during Roman times encounters, during the era of persections, the early Christian community. This story about the changes that came to Roman culture through early Christian witness chime with the Landscapes of Faith festival in June 2021, which comes out of the Library at Llantwit and celebrates stories of the faith traditions in the landscape of South Wales, including an exploration and marking of the deaths of Julius and Aaron at the Roman town of Caerleon, just north of the city of Newport. Little is known about the life and death of Julius and Aaron at this major Roman centre in the West of Britain, but their Christian witness was still remembered locally when Gildas recalls them during the 6th century in his book *On the Ruin of Britain*. Part of Newport today is still known as St Julian's. Glover's story of the dramatic persecutions and growing Christian witness, and how these affected a humble stonemason living in a Roman town, give us touching and scholarly insights from one of the large personalities of the early twentieth century. We see and feel the changing religious life of a small town under Roman rule and the beginnings and impulses of Christian art.

The last two chapters of *Vocation* were re-printed in Glover's 1921 collection of essays *The Pilgrim*[3] and I have included an

---

[3] T.R. Glover, *The Pilgrim*, Student Christian Movement, London 1921

appendix offering an essay from that collection, 'The Meaning of Christmas Day' along with a contemporary review by Howard Worsley of a more well-known book by Glover. I am very grateful to Dr Worsley for his contribution.

In presenting this lost text of *Vocation*, I have edited the language, shaping towards a more contemporary English, so that the energetic yet now slightly dated Edwardian style of Glover's original does not get in the way of his cherished subject to our modern ears. Any reader who would like to read Glover's slightly longer original can begin a treasure hunt to find a rare copy, or sometime call in to the Library at Llantwit to spend some pleasant hours reading, contemplating and enjoying the spectacular precincts and coastal scenery of the town.

R M Parry

JUNE 2021

THANKS

Grateful thanks to Edwin Counsell and Howard Worsley for their contributions to this volume and for their practical support for the Library at Llantwit project; thanks are offered to the congregation of St Illtud's church Llantwit Major for the forthcoming explorations and celebrations of the heritage of the church and town and their offer to visitors; we're very grateful to Elfed Evans and Celf Creative for the image of the Celtic cross at the Museum of Celtic Stones in the Galilee Chapel, Llantwit Major and to Michael Lindley of Truth Studio for the cover design.

VOCATION

Vocation

THE other day I came across some magazine article on the subject of "Choosing a Vocation". If words were not notorious for their uncertainty, one might feel surprise at such a phrase. If a vocation is a life's work to which one is called, how can one *choose* it? We may accept or reject a vocation, but we can hardly choose it. Yet the word is used idly, with little sense of its high meaning and history.

The theme of this book is Vocation, but approached from different points. It begins with a study of the work of Jesus, exploring purpose in his life. Secondly, it looks at how the call to share that work came to some of his earliest friends, and the impulse that brought them into it. After this we turn to Paul's understanding of what it means to serve Christ. This entails looking at how a person may belong to Jesus Christ and ways in which it is possible to serve Christ. Then we'll consider how vocation is a call to a person to use their gifts in a way that enables them to see where and when they are called to a new departure.

In summary, it all comes to this: the Christian vocation is dependent on a person's realization of what Jesus Christ has done, and continues to do, for him or her. Vocation is a realization of what Jesus Christ asks of that person. Vocation is service, and this requires a complete surrender of every part of a person's self in love and honesty. Vocation calls for the use of intellect, insight, sympathy, imagination, and it involves the gift for seeing what should be done without waiting for a precedent. Finally, vocation is accompanied by faith that the outcome of all work attempted for Christ is Christ's affair.

To some readers this may seem meaningless, insincere and conventional "church talk". But here it is suggested that if we touch the actual experience of the Christian church we will find these themes very real. We can discover that vocation is a living experience and the very gist and essence of life for men and women in our society. And in any case, this trying to understand vocation from the actual records of Christian life is honest and can do none of us much harm.

T R Glover

1

PURPOSE

IN THE LIFE OF JESUS

FOR Christian people everything begins with Jesus. Studying of the mind of Jesus is of signal importance, whether he is what the church has always claimed, Jesus Christ, or a man with supreme insight, or merely a great historical factor. It will be of no little significance then to set out to learn what was in his mind during the days of his ministry in Palestine.

Some people in churches have their attention focused on eschatology, claiming that Jesus lived chiefly in thoughts of a swift return to earth upon the clouds of heaven. More widely, many other people imagine that he was aiming for the embodiment of a gentle idealism in a well-balanced life of example. Or, as we shall ask, did he have before him a thoughtful purpose, which if not fully understood, in all events, was felt intensely.

IS JESUS PRINCIPALLY AN ESCHATOLOGICAL FIGURE?

The view has been strongly put before us in recent years that at the centre of the teaching of the historic Jesus is his eschatology. Confronted with failure he awaited or even precipitated the Passion, hoping that his generation should witness his triumphant return amongst clouds to inaugurate a Messianic reign, which he had taught was near. We are told that this is the moving force of this life and teaching.

It is quite clear that readers of the New Testament are liable to skip over eschatological sections that perplex them, along with other biblical passages, so there is merit in the vigorous and insistent call by some scholars to recall the historical Jesus. But it is not likely or desirable that these scholars should have everything their own way or they also will overlook things of importance.

In 132 AD, during the reign of the Hadrian, there was a Jewish revolt against the Romans led by a man called Bar-Cochba, who tried to establish some sort of Messianic kingdom. We will find a great difference between Bar-Cochba and Jesus, who was crucified under a Roman governor in the reign of Tiberius.

It is possible the proponents of a major eschatological focus in the life of Jesus have not studied the manner of his speech as well as the substance of it. Do words mean the same to thing to the person of genius as to a journalist? It is not clear that these eschatologically focused scholars realize to the full what Matthew Arnold meant when he said that "Jesus was above his reporters".

IS JESUS SIMPLY A PHILOSOPHIC TEACHER?

If we look for the gentle idealist of the well-balanced existence who saw life steadily and whole, and lived rhythmically, we will find that this is not the figure of Jesus in the Gospels. This gentle picture is more like Sophocles or Emerson. Jesus taught, and this teaching led to his crucifixion. His followers came to believe that Jesus was seated at the right hand of God, and from this position comes to judge the whole world, across all its history. He is not a gentle idealist.

THE MAIN EMPHASIS OF JESUS

We can ask questions about where the main emphasis of Jesus is located. And a good place to start is by looking at what he says. Let's begin with one of the most familiar parables,

> Then drew near unto him all the publicans and sinners. And the Pharisees and scribes murmured.

The wrong sort of people gathered around Jesus, and he strikes out a parable to them. You can imagine that it came to his mind with a sudden sweep of feeling. Perhaps it was a memory of boyhood, vivid and clear in detail of the quest and thrill of finding something, and now grown into an invitation to consider greater things.

> What man of you, having an hundred sheep, if he lose one of them, doth not leave the ninety and nine in the wilderness, and go after that which is lost, until he find it? And when he hath found *it*, he layeth *it* on his shoulders, rejoicing. And when he cometh home, he calleth together *his* friends and neighbours, saying unto them, Rejoice with me; for I have found my sheep which was lost.

This is how Luke tells the story. Matthew varies a few more touches,

> he goeth into the mountains and seeketh that which is gone astray

and adds,

> he rejoiceth more of that sheep than of the ninety and nine which went not astray

The parable that follows this concerns a coin which is lost and then found. It ends with a parallel phrase,

> There is joy in the presence of the angels of God over one sinner that repenteth

and this parable is followed by the parable of the Prodigal Son in which restorative rejoicing greets the return of the lost child.

Augustine in his *Confessions* devotes a chapter to these three parables.

> Oh, good God! What is it that happens in a man that he rejoices more in the deliverance of a soul despaired of and set free from greater danger, than if he had always had hope or the danger had been less? Yea, Thou also, Merciful Father, doest rejoice more over one penitent than over ninety-nine just persons, who need not repentance. And we also hear it with great delight, when we hear how the sheep which had gone astray is carried home on the exulting shoulders of the shepherd; and the drachma is restored to Thy treasures, while her neighbours rejoice with the woman who has found it; and the joy of the solemnity of Thy house brings tears, when in Thy house is read the story of the younger son, how 'he was dead and is alive again; he was lost and is found.'

> ... What, then, is it that happens in the soul when it is more delighted by the finding or recovery of things which it loves than if it had always had them?

And he gives a list of instances, in which everything cries out, "it is so!"

Why is it so? There are at least two answers.

9

We do not get the value of things when we see them lumped together in a mass. It is not until the separate thing is isolated and emphasised that we begin to grasp its significance and value. As we see it alone our attention is fixed on the thing, and we have a chance of realizing what it actually is, and appreciating its true value and meaning.

The fact of its being lost calls attention in a new way to the bond between the thing and you who own it. The thing was yours, and you knew it. But not with emphasis. And now you know it, and realise that beyond the intrinsic market value of the thing there is another value in its being *Meum*. It belongs to me.

That is the point that Jesus ushers in with his story of the lost sheep. It was one among a hundred. Its being lost has given it a new individuality. And now, its rescue has heightened that new individuality. It is now the sheep with a story, with associations of the long search. Every detail of the mountain in the long path outwards and the shorter, heavy-laden one in return belong to that sheep. This binds the sheep and shepherd together with an abundance of memories that are peculiar to them. It is not an experience that is exactly shared by any others, no matter how many in their turn are lost and found again. In the shepherd's sight the sheep are not items, but characters.

It has been shown in the past that the parables of Jesus rest on real, deep, practical examples and analogies. Not one of his parables is a fable. They are all aspects of the real. He appeals to facts.

Jesus asks whether this joy and celebration is real with the shepherd and his friends. He answers: Yes, it is. Then, he says,

> I say unto you, that likewise joy shall be in heaven over one sinner that repenteth, more than over ninety-nine just persons which need no repentance.

Can we believe this? For the re-birth of a single soul, and a poor one at that, is it not a great deal to ask us to believe there is such a celebration in the divine foundations?

And we must ask this question. Is it true? Because we have arrived at the very heart of Jesus. If it is not true then God perhaps falls short of what Jesus believed; and that is a statement not quickly to be ventured. In any case, this parable with its tremendous last words is the voice and teaching of Jesus. So what does he mean by the image of rejoicing in heaven? We don't commonly use this term, and we tend these days to stick to the verifiable. A poet may use a phrase like this about joy in heaven, but we are happier with prose and fact. This is a common complaint against the poet – that he or she does not see the facts. This complaint carries with it a suggestion that we, because we are down-to-earth and essentially prosaic, actually do see the facts. But really, if experience goes for anything, it is the other way around. The poet sees the facts first. And gradually other people see them. The down-to-earth person takes things in at a glance, and never gives another look. Truth does not surrender to such a careless attack.

Let us not be too quick in saying that Jesus was wrong because he says something we did not expect. He conceives that God is in the centre of a group of angels and has the most happiness. He conceives that God, as Augustine saw, rejoices more over the lost regained. In this way he emphasises Fatherhood of God and gives both terms, fatherhood and God, a new content.

Neither the word "God" nor "Father" means for us what Jesus intends, and because of this we hesitate over the lost sheep found. We, like the Stoics, conceive God as a kind of great Provincial Governor, a great statistician, who might feel a quiet satisfaction that the death-rate had fallen by a few percentage points, calling upon any angel who cared for statistics to share his satisfaction. And how many is a few percentage points of five billion people? Yes, God cares for the world. Yes, he cares for the Christian community, perhaps. But, for the individual? That is a great deal to say. Jesus said it and believed it, and he carried it out to the end.

We have to remember that Jesus faced the crowds of people who exist in the world and make us feel despair. He never courted them. They came about him hungry and diseased. He lived in the thick of the daily existence of people whom we might call today degenerates. Luke's gospel tells how Jesus on his last journey wept at the sight of Jerusalem. The city is the scene and focus of Israel's deepest emotions, highest hopes and most disastrous failures. The pilgrims throng before Jesus, turning the house of prayer into a den of thieves. It is, like every great pilgrim centre, a city of aspiration and blindness, of folly and sin, where Israel came to find God and killed God's prophets.

Jesus's attitude is always the same,

> The Son of Man came not to be ministered unto, but to minister, and to give His life a ransom for many… to seek and to save that which is lost.

What can he do? Jesus weeps over Jerusalem, and there is now only one thing left to do. He rides on and enters the city, deliberately, to be crucified.

That purpose runs through all. He makes this clear to his friends. He has a baptism to be baptized with. He has a cup to drink. He announces his death to his friends. He sets his face towards Jerusalem, for a prophet cannot be slain anywhere else, and as they go there together he leads the way and they follow in a strange mood of perplexity and embarrassment.

The end was not an accident. It was deliberate. He was to be a "ransom for many", and to give them rest, because every individual man, woman and child among them had his or her own meaning and significance for God. The life and death of Jesus turn upon this value of the last and least to God the Father. The last and the least have to be sought and found, and this is his method. He is to save women, men and children and ransom them and to do it by identification with them in suffering.

The Good Shepherd, as Christians were quick to see, is the type of Christ himself.

2

THE CALL FOR HELP

TWO striking moments in the life of Jesus must now claim our attention. They will enable us to link this central thought of Jesus with our subject of Vocation.

Matthew, in his gospel, describes how Jesus with his disciples made a great tour of villages and towns, teaching in synagogues, preaching the gospel of The Kingdom and healing every kind of sickness and disease. People are careless of what they see every day, and finally fail to see it. It falls upon the eye, but the eye does not mention it to the brain, or only in such a way that the brain ignores it. But a painter, or a poet, will see the familiar thing – and then it keeps breaking in every day with fresh significance upon the awareness of the person who knows the picture or poem, whether of happiness or pain.

Now in this journey with Jesus, we may say, the disciples probably saw little or nothing which they had not seen before, but they saw it in a new way altogether. It meant unspeakably now. Disease and sickness were not new things, but their re-action upon Jesus opened his friends' eye to them, and they began to see disease and sickness as he saw them. They would not touch a leper, a rule from the Old Testament writings in Leviticus, but Jesus did. So it was no idle quotation when later they applied to him the phrase from the biblical writings in Isaiah,

> Himself took our infirmities and bare our sicknesses.

Nor was it only with bodily sickness that they gained a new familiarity, for they began to see the isolation, loneliness and shame of men, women and cities as he saw it. They came to learn and know Jesus by identifying with him, as he identified himself with all he met.

Then came a great hour, when Jesus himself was seen with new eyes. They saw him watch the crowds, and they saw him moved as he watched. He used strong words about the crowds,

> They *fainted* and were *scattered abroad* as sheep having no shepherd

and, to be closer to the original Greek text, we might say that they were "worried and driven". The words must have been Jesus' own. They have in them a germ of a parable – a shepherdless flock, worried by dogs, driven helplessly hither and thither. Anyone who has lived in a sheep-rearing district knows what it means when a pair of dogs go out by night and slink back at dawn, leaving death and waste behind them.

One might call this the parable of the ninety-nine lost sheep. The world as Jesus saw it. It is a very different image to the ninety-nine righteous people who needed no repentance. Then he turns to his friends, and using another parable Jesus says,

> The harvest truly is plenteous, but the labourers are few; pray ye, therefore, the Lord of the Harvest that he will thrust forth labourers into his harvest.

The isolation, incoherence and misery of people means a ripeness for the message of God; the harvest is ripe and calls for reaping, the grain is falling where it stands for lack of reapers.

It seems to be the only time recorded when Jesus *asked* for the prayers of his friends. People are needed, and Jesus asks his friends to pray that they be sent – only people, but people who will work for him. He doesn't call for social machinery or great schemes of reformation, but plain people who are content not to be ministered unto, but to minister in his spirit for the people on behalf of whom he was giving his life. The name "Lord of the Harvest" implied a great deal, but let us think chiefly of Jesus asking for prayer, and prayer of this kind. Surely a call to prayer from his lips is a vocation.

A second passage which links the central thought of Jesus to the subject of Vocation belongs to a later stage of his ministry – the last evening together when Jesus and his friends shared a final supper before his crucifixion. Jesus uses words to Peter which receive little attention today, though readers of John Bunyan's book *Grace Abounding* have good cause to remember them. Jesus says,

> Simon, Simon, behold Satan asked to have you that he might sift you as wheat, but I prayed for thee, that thy faith might not fail, and thou, when thou art turned again, strengthen thy brethren.

The words seem to describe a scene, vivid before the eyes of Jesus as he spoke. As one studies these words other passages come to mind which fit with them. The words of Jesus constantly show how clearly he saw as he spoke. Every parable bears witness to that. But in one or two places we catch a glimpse of other scenes before his eyes – scenes that appear to be flashed upon him, as lightning in the night springs a countryside out of darkness upon the eyes, making it distinct in every detail.

In the temptation narrative we read how Satan showed Jesus all the kingdoms of the world in a moment of time, and in another passage of great interest and importance Jesus tells his friends,

> I beheld Satan as lightning fallen from heaven.

And now, in the words used at the final supper with his friends, we seem to be brought into a strange scene. Satan and Jesus are together in the same presence, each with a strong and urgent desire. It recalls the scenes in the beginning of the biblical writings of Job, and in Zechariah, where Satan comes before God with things to say to Him. In this last supper scene Satan is quite definite. He has a request which he pushes, for it is a strong verb; he "asked urgently for himself". This verb is so strong that the revisers of the text felt justified in printing in the margin, "or obtained you by asking". This is surely an impossible rendering here, but not out of the way in another connection.

The two then are, it would seem, in God's presence and Satan is earnestly asking for the disciple. And Jesus says,

> But I prayed for thee, that thy faith may not fail.

What a picture the words give! We saw Jesus in the previous passage asking for a prayer from his disciples; here we have a glimpse of him wrestling in prayer, and it seems that it took all the prayer-force he had, for the salvation of a single man. Indelible words, and indelible scene: the enemy of man pushing into God's presence for Peter's soul, and the Son of God at his prayers for Peter.

We read in the fourth gospel,

> Jesus, having loved His own which were in the world, loved them unto the end

and we can understand how people came to say this, when they remembered such a scene as Jesus shows us here at the last supper. And this thought stayed in the heart of the church, for Paul speaks of Jesus in this way,

> Who also make intercession for us,

and the author of the letter to the Hebrews writes similarly,

Seeing he ever liveth to make intercession for them

as if we needed the prayers of the ascended Christ, and had them.

Now, substitute for the word "Satan" and his request any form of words that will adequately capture the awful peril of the soul of a person, and then continue with the words that need no re-writing. The words of Jesus are so simple and good,

but I prayed for thee, that thy faith may not fail.

Let a person grasp that, and know that it is for them personally for whom Christ prayed in that awful hour of danger, and then realise that a request or command follows,

When thou art converted, strengthen thy brethren.

What will be the effect? It is possible that Jesus meant in speaking to Peter, "When you have come back to me." These are deeply moving words in view of all that followed in Peter's denial of having ever known Jesus.

Can any person realize vocation in any more compelling way than if it come in such a revelation of their life's utmost need, and of Jesus personal prayer, backed by a request for such earnestness and tenderness?

All this I did for thee.

These words of Jesus are the constant thought of the Christian church. And if the gospels are to be taken at all seriously, Jesus did more for Peter than pray for him. Anyone with a heart to understand what Jesus did for Peter will find it much. And Jesus did and does as much for every one of us.

3

THE STIGMATA OF JESUS

St Paul ends his letter to the Galatian Christian community with a strong and striking phrase,

> From henceforth let no man trouble me, for I bear branded on my body the marks of Jesus

- the stigmata of Jesus.

The stigmata borne by Francis of Assisi and others may be familiar to you – marks on brow and side, on hands and feet, like the scars of wounds produced by some intense concentration of the mind on the sufferings of Jesus. They come at times to people of a certain type when, following Jesus, they have entered into what Paul calls "the fellowship of his sufferings".

But the marks on Paul's body were of a much more ordinary nature. We have only to glance at the account of his adventures which he gives in his letter to the church at Corinth to realize that his body must be covered with scars of one kind and another. Elsewhere he tells us he "buffets" his body, and he carries about in the body the dying of the Lord Jesus.

If, as seems more likely, we adopt a position called the "South Galatian" theory and hold the idea that Paul's letter to the church in Galatia was sent to Paul's friends and converts along the great Southern Road through Asia Minor – at Antioch, Iconium, Lystra and Derbe – then a curious consideration arises. Some of the readers of the letter, or those who listened to it when it was read out, must have remembered vividly as they reached this sentence a night when some of those scars were open wounds, and they had attended to the healing of them. Some may even have been among those who threw the stones and made the scars – people whose Christian life began, like Paul's, at the stoning of an apostle.

Now Paul looks at his scars and a metaphor rises in his mind. In the Roman Empire, when a slave ran away, if he was caught his owner might have him stripped, the irons heated, and the letters F V G (*fugitivus*) branded on him. Perhaps the owner's initials might be burnt upon the slave, too.

This practice long survived in France where convicts were branded 'V" (*voleur*) or 'T F' (*travail forcé*) and people took children to see the branding done as a lesson in virtue.

The historian Herodotus suggests a further line of thought, for he tells us that in Egypt if a slave were dissatisfied with his master he might go to the temple of Herakles and take on him the stigmata of the god, and be free for ever of his master and belong to the god. Such marks were indelible. There are in Greek quite a number of words connected with the branding of slaves.

When Paul, then, says of himself that branded upon his body he has the stigmata of Jesus he uses a very strong figure of speech, and it was one that was familiar to his friends because four of Paul's letters begin with the phrase,

Paul, the slave of Jesus Christ.

He lived in a world where society was organised throughout on the basis of slavery. It is obvious that he knew what the word implied, and when he used it, he meant it.

Juvenal, the Roman poet, wrote

PONE CRUCEM SERVO! ITA SERVUS HOMO EST?

"Crucify this slave! Is a slave a man?" The master or mistress could do very much what they liked with their property – humanity was hardly reckoned in a slave. The Stoic approach to life would not have taken so much trouble to establish the principle that slaves were also human if people had not thought so, or had not acted on the thought. A slave was a piece of property – legal property – and a branded slave was marked as the property of another.

This is Paul's metaphor. He is the slave of Jesus, and is branded with his marks,

> Whose I am and Whom I serve.

The branding was a mark of shame. No man was branded of his own free will – apart from slaves taking on them such a brand as that of Herakles which was to exchange one servitude for another. To be the slave of Jesus Christ had not been Paul's intention. The shame of bearing Christ's name – of being "made as the filth of the world and the off-scouring of all things" – the loss of home and family and friendships, of everything – the squalid life of privation, insult, persecution and danger – humiliation from beginning to end …. no person would have chosen it, and Paul did not choose it. It was a vocation.

> Necessity is laid upon me; yea, woe is unto me if I preach not the gospel! For if I do this thing willingly, I have a reward: but if against my will, I am entrusted with a stewardship,

he writes in the letter to his friends in Corinth. A steward was very often a slave, if not always. Paul is at the beck and call of another whom he never chose to make his Master. He must have no will of his own.

> Go into the city and it shall be told of thee what
> thou must do

is the instruction heard by Paul in the account of his conversion, given in the biblical account of the activity of the early church. So far was he from choosing a vocation, he has to wait for his orders.

This life of obedience extends into the realm of thinking. He speaks of the warfare of the soul, bringing down "calculations" or "imaginations" and

> taking captive every thought into the obedience of
> Christ.

When one reads his letters with any attention to his modes of thought, it is clear that this must have meant struggle. The extraordinary quickness of his thought is noticeable in the strange and flashing tangents at which he moves. Witness the play with Yes and No in the second letter to Corinthian friends, and the splendid drive which makes Jesus the Yes of all the promises of God.

Or again, remark the intensity with which he thinks and sees. He was a man, one would judge, of passionate friendships, liable to feel solitude peculiarly. Paul misses his friend Titus and so has "no rest for his soul" in the region of Greek settlements of Troas even though "a door is opened of the Lord". When he goes to Macedonia and finds Titus he writes,

thank God who always makes us triumphant in
Christ.

Or take Paul's use of the Greek verb *perisseuô* and similar
words. It is translated in English by words like
"abundant". He is a man for whom everything lives and
moves, for whom everything means intensely. And
everything is quick and rapid.

Such a temperament is not all gain. It has its other side,
and when we find Paul explaining to friends at Philippi
how the peace of God can "keep our hearts and
thoughts," it surely gives some hint as to the battle it cost
to bring thoughts so quick and independent into
subjection. These thoughts are to be ruled even in solitude
and prison, and to be content there. Let a person see what
can be done in battle with his or her imagination and he
or she will know. This is Paul's struggle. People of easier
natures will not guess how hard a man of many interests
and warm sympathies may find it to realize Christ's part
in all, or how hard it is for him to feel sure that Christ has
His own place among the interests.

Thought and act are at God's disposal, and a short study
of Paul's life will show how closely bound up it is with
indications of God's will. He is "forbidden of the Holy
Ghost to speak the word in Asia"; he would go into
Bithynia, but "the spirit of Jesus suffered them not"; there
is a call to Macedonia; in Corinth he must stay and not be
afraid.

In every place the work is the same – to preach the Gospel. There are two sides to this, and they are not always fully realized. Paul was a man of education, a man of clear head and wide range, a Hebrew of Hebrews, and a Roman citizen. And when he came to the Christian Church he found there "not many wise men", nor many mighty or noble – mostly the foolish things of the world, the weak and base, the despised. For a man of quick mind and culture it would not be easy at all times to be entirely at home with his new company. Nor would it be easy for a man who understood Jewish prejudice and Greek cleverness to go to Jew and Greek with a gospel which they found "a stumbling block" and "foolishness", and well knowing what a fool they thought him to preach

> Jesus Christ, and him crucified

to the stiff-necked Jew and to the Greek, witty and shallow. How contemptuous the "little Greek" might be is shown us by Juvenal's writing. Paul's business is to go to them with that which will rouse the anger of the Jew and the snigger of the Greek. And he knows exactly what his reception will be; but he has to go. He says,

> Necessity is laid upon me.

But here another consideration comes in. He says in writing to the Romans,

> Who art thou that judges another man's servant? ... to his own master he standeth or falleth

and then in his quick way, with a flash of thought, he adds,

> Yea, he shall be holden up.

The passage at the end of the Galatian letter with which we began bears the same sense,

> Let no man trouble me; I bear on my body the stigmata of Jesus.

The responsibility for the message rests with the Master, not with the slave. The one is bound, the other is free; and if the Master is satisfied with the delivery of the message, who else can speak?

Now that we have reached the Master one or two more factors appear which have to be considered. The beginning of it all was not, as we have seen, Paul's wish or choice,

> It pleased God, who set me apart even from my mother's womb, and called me by His grace, to reveal His Son in me, that I might preach Him among the heathen.

God chose him – upset every plan he had made for his life – set him to the hardest and most shameful of tasks – and all in virtue of a revelation of love that went beyond belief. The life is impossible but for the love of God in Christ, and with it is inevitable,

> The love of Christ constraineth us.

It is the power that broke his life, made a slave of him, and branded him; it is the message, the debt to Greek and to barbarian; it is the impulse, and the new life, though he dies daily – the pledge and assurance that his labour is not in vain in the Lord, that he is not alone, but Christ works in him,

Who shall separate us from the love of Christ?

And there it is every day with him to the end, as it was promised. If we wish to have Paul's account of Vocation it lies in our hand on every page he writes.

It is worthwhile to note how greatly Paul emphasizes the other side of ownership – the responsibility of the Master to his servant, and how his sense of this rests upon experience. He has a "thorn in the flesh", as we remember, and prays to have it taken away. The prayer was not answered, as some people would say, because the "thorn", whatever it was, remained. But the promise is given,

My grace is sufficient for thee

and Paul is content – he can "boast" in weakness now – and does it with delight, for in them he grows conscious of the powers of Christ resting upon him. The same note prevails throughout this line in his letter to the church in Rome,

nay, but in all these things we are more than conquerors through Him that loved us.

As Paul's life is more and more entirely at the service of Christ, his knowledge deepens of what Christ can do and be. The two responsibilities go together; the servant is responsible to the Master, and the Master to the servant. The very stigmata themselves become so many promises. The body is marked all over with signs of the master's use, as a favourite book which a person reads often shows most signs of wear – pencilled in here and there, crushed, worn and shabby, and in all these things identified with the reader who cannot do without it. The battered body and the tried and weary spirit are reminders themselves to Paul that "Christ liveth in me." The "fellowship of sufferings" belongs to fellow-workers; a fresh seal upon their union.

The responsibility of the Master extends to the result of the work done. "Duties are ours, while results are God's," it has been said. And that again is included in Paul's view of service.

Your labour is not in vain in the Lord.

A person may be dissatisfied with the scant achievement he attains, the small outcome of his work, or his complete failure. How does he know what it means? Is the servant always in his Master's secret? "Let no man trouble me" – not even myself, says Paul– "I bear in my body the stigmata of the Lord Jesus."

But, in conclusion, to return to the original metaphor, Paul's experience suggests a more general reflection. In all art and literature, in every great and new creation, the impulse seems to lie in a new and vivid experience which makes a new knowledge. The person branded "F V G" knew something of those letters of the alphabet in quite a different way from all the rest. A burning experience and a burning memory indelible from flesh and spirit gave those letters. It is somehow so that the poets learn their own peculiar alphabet – something is burnt upon the person, perhaps in pain, perhaps in joy, for the joy of insight may go with pain and overwhelm it – and you get a new person. All knowledge is changed for this person. They knew before – no, they thought they knew – but now they know – not so many things, but the one thing in a new way that alters all.

> If any person be in Christ, it is a new creation

says Paul. All things are made new. They have new values in the new light, and none is ever again what it was before. It cannot be. Life has a new intensity, a new direction, a new purpose. It becomes a vocation.

> I know in whom I believed

wrote Paul.

Much is said today about the prospects of Christianity; of re-construction and re-statement. Can it be true that certain things in the Christian fabric will stand no strain, that there is no "grouting" possible here, but the whole must be taken down and rebuilt without them? Or is it that we need a new vocabulary?

One thing is more and more clear. The real need is not to reconstruct or to restate but to re-experience. A touch of what burnt the stigmata into Paul – and how clear and living a lost and dead language becomes! How it lets one into a new world of reality, where men and women are living in a new creation, passed from death unto life, full of a new song, every day, "more conquerors through Him that loved us," and gloriously sure of the highest of all vocations, "ambassadors for Christ."

4

THE MINISTRY

MINISTRY, as we saw, was one of the avowed purposes in the life of Jesus, and we find again that it gives the keynote for the life of Paul – "the slave of Jesus Christ." In the second letter to his friends at Corinth, Paul discusses the ministry of a servant of Christ. The fourth chapter of his letter begins,

> Having therefore this ministry.

We have seen how Paul came to be a minister of Christ. In this letter he explains the nature and methods of this ministry, and in the third chapter he speaks of

> us who are the ministers of a new covenant.

That is a particularly interesting phrase which comes from the prophet Jeremiah, and it is worthwhile to see how he reached it. The prophet Jeremiah is, on the whole, a failure, as indeed he told the LORD at the very moment of his call he was sure to be. The people will not listen to him, and he has a terrible type of message given to him for them – the announcement of God's judgements – it is not a task he would have chosen, yet to this was he called.

At one point Jeremiah speaks out of one judgement after another doomed to come; and then he breaks out with a sudden passionate cry, that seems to have little immediate connection with the rest of the chapter,

> Oh! earth, earth, earth, hear thou the word of the Lord!

It was as if he was weary – and God weary – of messages of judgement, and cried in passion to the world and to people:

> If only you would listen in time.

Slowly he comes to understand that this unhappy state of things cannot last forever; as sure as God is God, a day must come when there will be a new relationship between God and man. Jeremiah says, a little later,

> In that day, saith the Lord, I will make a new covenant.

My attention was first directed to this passage in Jeremiah when I was working on the scheme of "proof" texts used by writers in the Early Church. They turned to the Old Testament looking for every text that by its natural meaning, or by any possible or impossible unnatural meaning, referred to the future Christian gospel. They went to this chapter of Jeremiah again and again, until the reference, Jeremiah, chapter 29, verse 31 was familiar to me.

The prophet Jeremiah, judged by popular standards, was a failure; but his book and his great prophecy lived. How quickly this passage was caught up by Christian readers we do not know, but Paul has it very early in Christian history. When the Christian books and writings were finally gathered together, Jeremiah's phrase lent itself as a title for the collection, and this best-known volume in the world is called the New Testament.

This phrase Paul uses, and it is worth study. His ministry is essentially that of the new covenant, the new dispensation, from which Jeremiah's prophecy that began with the words,

I have loved thee with an everlasting love

is to be fulfilled - all shall know God from the least to the greatest, when He will forgive their iniquity and remember their sin no more. If Paul calls this ministry a little more modestly the 'ministry of righteousness' it is with good authority, but we will not gather all his meaning until we realise the thrill the word 'righteousness' carries for Paul.

'Righteousness' had been the passion of his former Pharisee life, he had tried to work it out and failed; and now, "not having my own righteousness" he finds another's righteousness that is given to him. The unity of Paul's life is bound up with the concept of righteousness, before and after his conversion; and when he speaks of the ministry of righteousness, it is no dull or conventional word for him.

We have to allow the word the meaning he gave it, if we are to understand him; and it is a glad meaning that makes his heart beat. He has been entrusted with a ministry that is, as he tells us in his letter to Corinth, "glorious".

Then at the end of the fifth chapter of this letter the whole thing is summed up in still more splendid phrase.

> All things are of God, who hath reconciled us to Himself by Jesus Christ, and hath given to us the ministry of reconciliation; to wit, that God was in Christ, reconciling the world to Himself, not imputing their trespasses unto them; and hath committed us unto the word of reconciliation. Now then we are ambassadors for Christ, as though God did beseech you by us: we pray you in Christ's stead, be ye reconciled to God.

Here he touches the ministry in its most recognisable aspect. For the world's quarrel with God is notorious. People are angry with God for the way in which He handles their lives. There is too much wrong with our circumstances, too much amiss with the world; it should have been made otherwise.

We know that ourselves. But in the heathen world things are far more difficult between people and God; if God, singular or plural, would only let people alone and be done with it – but God or the Gods will not, and life is a long struggle in the dark, full of suspicion, fear and soreness. To people bitter in this quarrel the Christian is sent with a message of goodwill - overtures from God towards reconciliation. The phrase is Paul's, but the whole Christian church will confirm it.

Once again we touch Vocation – and no slight conception of it.

But how does a person become fit for such a calling? Paul touches on this in the opening sentence of the fourth chapter. The calling and ministry comes out of a new personal relation with God, and this new personal relation continues throughout. His vocation is not an abstract realization of duty. It is not as if he'd had the weighty sense that something ought to be said or done if only he could think what it was – as it so often is with us today. Paul is far simpler and clearer. His ministry is the outcome of relations with Jesus Christ, and it has all the force and power of a personal passion. An abstract appeal never grips like a personal one. Men and women will sacrifice themselves for love of family group or country, but the more general need of humanity does not appeal very strongly to most of us. It did appeal to Paul. He felt an obligation to preach the gospel to Greeks and barbarians. For real effective service of men and women the love of Jesus, which frankly was Paul's motive, has nothing that approaches its power.

> As we have received mercy...

He strikes at once the personal note. He and God have met in Christ; God is shining in his heart now; there is something in the past that has been blotted out; the failure of his life has been taken away; the law of sin and death within him has been broken down, nailed to the Cross, finished and done with – and none of this was easy, as Paul well saw; there is a new law of righteousness, a fulfilment of his old passion for righteousness in the sight of God. And all this is given him once and forever, and every day anew, by the unimaginable love and goodness and mercy of God in Christ. The whole basis and fabric of life are changed, and Paul has escaped from the painful old life where self was the centre, and he has found a new centre in Christ "who loved me and gave himself for me".

A few words of Luther may be quoted from his commentary on Paul's letter to the Galatians, and upon discovering Luther's words, John Bunyan said that he read of his own personal condition

> so largely and profoundly handled, as if his Book
> had been written out of my heart.

Such a thing is possible because Luther's text gives Paul's sense with great vigour, and it is reinforced for us by the experience of Luther himself, and of Bunyan, as he tells us,

Christ when he cometh, is nothing else but joy and sweetness to a trembling and broken heart, as here Paul witnesseth, who setteth him out with his most sweet and comfortable title, when he saith: *which loved me and gave himself for me.* Christ therefore in very deed is a lover of those which are in trouble and anguish, in sin and death, and such a lover as gave himself for us: who is also our High Priest, that is to say a mediator between God and us miserable and wretched sinners. What could be said (I pray you) more sweet and comfortable to the poor afflicted conscience? ... Read therefore with great vehemencie these words *Me* and *for Me.*

The thing is as individual as Paul and Luther can make it – a personal relation between Paul and God in Christ, and a deliberate choice of Paul by Christ for a particular service. It was God's good pleasure to choose him. What a picture of a Christian vocation! God, with all the resources of omnipotence at His disposal, chooses Saul of Tarsus – and not him alone.

If one has taken up the Christian position at all it is hard to escape the inference that, in view of that personal relation which is the gist of the gospel, some such individual ministry falls to every one of us - or else, as Luther says in the passage quoted above, "the gospel must be nothing but a fable."

What a thing it is for a man or woman to know that God has deliberately picked him or her for a piece of work, as a person who God knew he could trust! What must it be to have this thought alive in one's heart that God picked *me*

Read with great vehemencie this word ME

- individually and personally set *me* to this work because then He knew it was safe to be done! That lies in Paul's words.

The real difficulty in in all schemes of life, or reform, or progress, is the motive. Paul, however, has no doubt about it – "the love of Christ constraineth us," - literally, holds us into it. There is the path, and there is the work, and nothing else is possible, for the love of Christ keeps him there.

Duty is a great word, and altruism ought to be; but, when all is said and done, historically there is nothing that takes men and women into service of the deepest and truest kind and keeps them at it with energy and courage, that can compare with the motive that St Paul gives here. And when the Christian Church is not quite sure about this, all its service shows the effects of its hesitation.

At this point it may be worthwhile to pause for a moment and remember to what sort of life the love of Christ may constrain. "Constraineth" here means to hold tight and to guide. The life of the missionary in the lands of the tropics is often very humdrum – a round of discomfort, periodic sickness and disappointment, everlasting shortness of means, danger and sometimes horrible danger – it is not a life to choose; but the love of Christ may leave a person no choice. Christ wishes this done, and a wish between people who love each other is enough. This is the story of Christian missions from Antioch till today.

Paul uses a very interesting phrase,

> Our ambition is to be well pleasing to Him

It is the mirror image in reverse of "love constrains". Paul has given up everything to please Him – has "suffered the loss of all things" – and now the one ambition of his life is to please Him. Elsewhere, in Paul's letters, he uses the same idea, illustrating it with the soldier whose aim is to please the general who enlisted him, to whom he has sworn service and allegiance.

It is perfectly plain that it is not always so with Paul. People of his character, of the active quick mind, of energy and invention, people with careers open to them, do not readily throw away ambition – not even when they enter the service of Christ – for it is an insidious thing. A man of Paul's character may wish to do his service of Christ in a way that will please himself – to choose his task, perhaps. Or even when he loyally does not choose it, but accepts it, he may wish like an artist to get a certain finish into his work – the clean, clear, delicate touch which must be there if the work is to be personally satisfying; and to leave a thing half-finished for Christ's sake is sometimes a hard and bitter thing, even if the work itself had never any other motive than to please Christ.

It is possible to have a divided allegiance between Christ and his work. It is hard to suppress ambition, but over and over again Paul does suppress it, until the old ambition dies away from constant cutting down, and the new one has room to grow – the one desire to please Him.

Once again it is the personal connection

> He loved me and gave Himself for me

and

> to please Him.

There is no pleasing an abstract idea or principle. The force of gravity is not pleased, however much one humours it with the care with which the cup is set on the table. No one ever pleased maternity or paternity, but a mother and father are fortunately not abstract nouns – they are very concrete and common, and much easier to please. Service is a different thing when it has the motive of pleasing someone who loves us. Service is of course possible on the basis of abstract principle (and whether it really *is* abstract is open to question), and it was such service that the Roman Emperor and philosopher Marcus Aurelius gave to the world.

Unconscious of the origin of compassion, we may yet love our fellow men and women in a sort of way and try to serve them – and love them at least in the plural, or in the noun of "multitude", which signifies "many but not much" – but how one wishes these people were different!

But with Paul's motive impossible people become possible. The love of Christ compels; we must re-think some people.

Supposing now that a person is committed to the service of Jesus Christ, and has a vocation, what methods should be employed?

"We faint not," says Paul in the established translation, meaning that there is no giving way, no slacking in energy. The life that is moved by a passion like Paul's – passion that burns and glows – will not be hindered by a faint heart. There's plenty to trouble Paul; perplexities, tribulations, persecutions, fightings, and fears, the care of all the churches[4].

He is "cast down," "always bearing about in the body the dying of the Lord Jesus" – but not one of these things moves him, and he presses to the mark. Of course, Paul was naturally a man of purpose and energy, as he showed clearly in his persecuting days, but now as an Apostle he has not the human backing that the persecutor had. He relies, as he avows, on strength ministered from a higher source.

---

[4] Editor's note: What a phrase! – "the care of all churches". Which Christians think like that today? Where are the Christian communities or people whose vocation is "the care of all churches"?

He goes on to speak of the earnest sincerity that is asked of a person entrusted with a stewardship by Jesus Christ. Sincerity is not so easy a task as some people think; it is not easy at all to be sure that one tells the truth, even if one tries, either to others or to oneself. There are those who hold bluntly that the essence of Christianity is deliberate self-deception – this criticism is not very historical, for if character is ever to be read at all, it is plain that in few societies have there been so many persons as in the Christian church diaphanously candid with themselves, in self-criticism and in apprehension of truth.

We have renounced the hidden things of shame,

says Paul. One might hardly have expected such a statement from a character so strong and pure; it sounds like a confession; but the chapters from his second letter are full of the thought of the awful openness of the life of the Christian.

We have been made manifest to God,

he says, thrown open, seen through and through by God; we must all some day be thrown open and manifested before the judgement seat of Christ; and we aim at being open and manifest to men and women here and now,

commending ourselves to every person's conscience in the sight of God

with God looking on, knowing our secrets if we have any. You feel this to be a picture of life where all the windows of the soul are thrown open, where the sun searches every corner of the room.

Today we tend to speak of "sin" in a pathological way, and to be more impressed with the pathology of sin than with the guilt of it. The germ metaphor for sin is not quite unfamiliar in the New Testament. Paul's method, one might say, is the modern one – to throw open the windows to air and sun and have "God shining in our hearts."

Openness of life and no secrets – if a person is to serve Christ that person must be open for everyone to see into, and see through; and if there is anything wrong it seems better that it should be known by everyone at once. One day everyone will know, Paul feels, before the judgement seat of Christ,

on the day when God judges the secrets.

The same frankness is to characterise all dealings with all people. It has been pointed out that, in writing to people at Corinth, Paul uses several commercial terms; and one of them is here,

not tricking the Word of God, not huckstering it.

The Greek word used is very striking, translating as "trying the tricks of a retail trader on it". It represents Greek outlook and Greek experience of the trader. The word comes from the vocabulary of the small shopkeeper in the bazaar. The Christian apostle will not "boom his goods", he will not dress up his message; he will neither tone it down nor touch it up; and there will be, Paul implies, no attempt at rhetoric or at putting the thing in what might be supposed to be the right way.

John Bunyan knows this and writes in the preface to his book *Grace Abounding*,

> I could have stepped into a style much higher than this in which I have here discoursed, and could have adorned all things more than I have seemed to do; but I dare not: God did not play in tempting of me; neither did I play, when I sank, as into a bottomless pit, when the Pangs of Hell caught hold upon me; wherefore I may not play in relating of them, but be plain and simple, and lay down the thing as it was.

Paul has the same principle – he will "use great plainness of speech" and sincerity. In his previous letter he says the same: "not with enticing words of wisdom", and he renounces everything but his message,

> I determined not to know anything among you except Jesus Christ and Him crucified.

I think it is the same method used by Paul in Athens, for his purpose was the same there – only in Athens a different dialect is spoken. "In weakness and fear and much trembling," and with no aid from the school of rhetoric, he endeavours to tell a plain tale – well knowing, as we saw, with what feelings of anger and ridicule it will be received – and telling it all the same. And in the end it proved to be "with demonstration of the spirit and power."

Any person may fortify his or her reason with argument against the Christian faith. It is always possible to find arguments equally good for and against everything, if you do not wish to come to close quarters. But conscience is not so defended, and while it is immune when rhetoric is employed against it, it will yield to the earnest direct truthfulness which Paul describes.

As of sincerity, as of God, we speak in Christ.

It does not need to be good speaking. There is on record a revival of religion in a church, which began with a sermon that was a fiasco. It had been prepared, but it broke down; and that fact apparently threw people back into finding out the cause. Working back into the minister's mind in a new way altogether, they came up against a great motive and a great inspiration; and from that some of them gained their first insight into the love of Christ. It is curious how often the possession of great gifts is fatal to the accomplishment of what they might achieve. Charm, after all, is the most potent thing in the world, and love and simplicity are two of its chief constituents. Once it is clear to people that a person is genuinely influenced and controlled by the love of Jesus Christ, that person becomes a real force – very often quite beyond his or her intellectual gifts.

But this is not where Paul leaves the ministry. It is "treasure in brittle vessels" as John Wycliffe translates it, "that the excellency of the power may be of God and not of us."

All things are of God,

he emphasizes. God has given us the "earnest of the spirit," so that "we are always confident." God gives his people something that lives, moves and works, and is real in the experience of men and women. If we tried to define it – whatever success we achieved in the task, we should have to give up our definition as the real thing grew upon us.

God gives us guidance. God gives words, and sometimes he takes words away and says things over our heads – and how it is all done no Christian knows, but knows that it is so. God gives all, when once we are in Christ. If anyone thinks this unlikely – it is very unlikely, but there is no other account that Christians have to give of their experience.

To sum up, there is the world with its quarrel against God, keeping Him out of its life; and there is the Christian, with God shining in his or her heart, entrusted with the ministry of reconciliation and of the love of Christ. The contrast is Vocation itself.

5

THE TALENTS

ONE of the outstanding differences between Christianity
and other religions is the small space given to maxims and
rules and methods of Jesus and his more sympathetic
followers. This is one of the difficulties of a Christian
vocation – you have to find out very often for yourself
what to do, by bringing to bear upon a situation whatever
faculty you have of consecrated sense and imagination.

All work, according to Carlyle, is an appeal from the seen
to the unseen. All relation with men and women implies
divination; our daily relations with friend and pupil
depend upon imagination and sympathy; without these
prayer and all other work for Christ are almost
inconceivable.

In every sphere of human life, where things really matter,
one of the first great dangers is dullness. The

unimaginative in social discourse or in family life becomes impossible. In the sphere of religion it is incalculable what is lost when this faculty of grasping the fact in its life and significance is wanting.

It is interesting to turn to the gospels and see how often Jesus, our Lord, is struck with the absence of insight that men display. The gospel of Mark abounds in instances of the disciples themselves shocking Jesus by want of faith and intelligence.

> To you it is given to know the mysteries,

he says, and they do not know them – they ought to see, but they only half see and only half realize. With the outside world it is the same,

> Go and tell John what things ye see and hear.

The Pharisees and others are directed to look upon the ordinary signs of sky and cloud and are bidden to see in them an analogy. Life is full of significance if you will only look at it – what else is needed?

Not to pursue the subject over too wide a field, let us turn to the parable in which Jesus draws the danger of the slack or dull imagination – the parable of the Talents or the Pounds. Its bearing upon our general subject of Vocation hardly needs to be pointed out, nor is it his only parable that turns on the use of opportunity, on debt, and responsibility.

It comes like a page of contemporary history. Members of royal and noble houses in the eastern Mediterranean were constantly going to Rome to secure if they could, by negotiation, bribery or other means, thrones and kingdoms. The "certain nobleman" in Luke's version of the parable may quite well have been Herod – he has some traits of the family very strongly marked. Here, as he constantly does, Jesus draws from life and his detail, if sometimes not to be pressed into double meanings, illuminates the story and makes it come alive.

The Herod, then, of the parable goes to Rome, and everybody knows why; and "his citizens" – not yet his subjects, but his fellow citizens – send an embassy after him with all speed, hoping it may arrive in time to prevent mischief. They plead,

> We do not wish to be this man's subjects,

It must often have happened so. Meantime the Herod has left his estates and servants behind, planning with care what he wants done in his absence. He has no friends, very possibly; the only people in whom he can trust are his servants – freedmen and slaves – and he picks them for their work "according to their several ability." These servants must live and do their work in a hostile community, in an environment of mistrust and hate, working for an absent master who may return a broken and disappointed man, or may never return at all.

But the master does return, and comes as King, and the situation is acutely changed. He is now absolute master of the country, kingdom, tetrarchy or whatever it is, by the fiat of the Roman Emperor, and he has to govern it. Governing in his vocabulary means keeping the country quiet and squeezing the utmost possible out of it. He has no civil service on which to rely; everything needs a fresh start. There may be underlings who can be retained; what he wants is viziers, high ranking executive officials, and he can look nowhere except to his own household – to the freedmen and slaves whom he has had all along – and it is a matter of urgency to know who he can trust. It has never been so important to him to be absolutely sure of the character of his people – they may have their faults and vices, but he must be able to be sure of their loyalty, their energy and their intelligence. They must be the people to see instantly what is to be done – to foresee and forestall what hostile persons or groups will do – they must be people of insight and action. So, he holds his enquiry.

In another parable we have an instance of the servant who simply dismissed his master from mind and lived for the moment, eating and drinking in riot and disorder – and his case is soon settled. But in this present parable we have the "good and faithful" servants, and we see the relief and satisfaction with which the master hails the discovery of their quality. They are his people who have worked steadily and faithfully in a hostile and critical environment – who have learned to watch and to venture, and who have sturdily identified themselves with their master and believed in his future. His praise of them is swift and lavish, and ready to hand he has for each of them a vast new opportunity, which will mean at once work on a larger scale and reward out of proportion to all they have done.

But the servant with the single talent is the man upon whom Jesus has spent most care in telling his story. Jesus draws this servant with an individuality not given to the more faithful servants. That these others have character is implied by the whole narrative; but, as Jesus groups his picture, the two faithful servants stand, as it were, on each side of their master – they are figures worthy of our study indeed – but the centre is held by this new King and this curiously drawn servant of his. It is as if Jesus meant us to study the servant with closer interest.

This man, the servant with one talent, is not a bad servant like the drunken and wasteful slave of the other parable. He has a sense of responsibility, and he certainly has an eye for character. The servant makes it quite clear that he understands the Herod type – he sketches it accurately to the life – and in the conclusion of the story we see through the King's words and acts, in his treatment of this servant and of the enemies who sent the embassy to Rome, that the servant was quite right in his assesment of his master, as far as it went.

But the servant with one talent never realizes what his knowledge implies. He knows the value of property, but he does not see that this connotes its use. He lacks energy, and he will not take risks; and he does not see that his safe line of conduct keeping the treasure absolutely intact and secure from loss means simply the depreciation of the treasure and this is the very loss he is guarding against. If the servant's character assessment of his master is right, how can he expect the master to be satisfied without the interest his wealth should bring him?

But the servant fails in another way. As a critic of his master, shrewd as he is, he fails (as shrewd critics often do) by missing the large and generous traits in his master's character – the warm and glowing praise his master can give, and that keen appreciation of capacity which is the mark of the man of action. The servant does not see what great features there are in this hard, exacting and cruel Herod. He did not see the future of his master – did not believe in the kingdom to be – missed the vast possibilities. And now – of what use is he?

He has shown that he cannot be trusted with the work most urgent to be done – what sort of vizier would he be with his prudential half-views, his inability to see a situation and thereupon to act on it – his reluctance to commit to any action that implies faith either in the future or his master? The swift and incisive Herod is done with him, in a word, and turns headlong to his next business, which, as it happens, is that blending of vengeance and prudence that made so large a part of king-craft - there is action and insight once more in this man of force.

The unfaithful servant, as we call him, fails, as we fail, through the slack imagination. He knows and he sees – yes, he knows and he sees – but as Jesus, our Lord, says elsewhere, "seeing he sees not and does not understand." Why does our Lord draw him with such care?

The drift of the parable is clear enough in many ways – it concerns the use of the talent entrusted, whether money, capacity or charm; it handles the seriousness of work for the absent master, and the amazing return such work can yield, in immediate result, in praise from above, in incredibly magnified opportunity; the awful doctrines, persistent throughout the New Testament, of the loss of unused faculty and of sin working out in depravation of the effective elements of nature and character; and the rejection of the unfit, which is something we are apt to overlook these days.

But, behind all of this, what does Jesus mean by the pains he has taken in drawing that character? Is it not, taken with similar suggestions abundant in his teaching, a warning against the realization of things by halves – a warning against the danger which is clear everywhere, but in the most serious sphere of all, the spiritual, an infinitely more significant danger of being content with an unrealized life?

Let us look at ourselves. Goethe has a passage, quoted by Carlyle, about weaning ourselves from the half-life, and coming to live in the whole, good, gentle and resolute,

> Uns vom Halben zu entwohnen
> Und im Ganzen, Guten, Schonen
> Resolut zu leben.

What of the Christian life? What of unrealized opportunity, of unrealized sin, of good and evil half-known and accepted lazily – "all that sort of thing" – as we carelessly say? Is such a life life at all before the bright, keen eyes of the Teacher of Nazareth?

Or again, what of an unrealized Christ, known more or less and left in half-knowledge? Is not the weakness of our modern Christianity this – that we are content with the slack imagination, with sheer half-knowledge where Christ is concerned – that we do not grasp him, nor understand him, nor use him, nor love him to the full? And yet the love of Jesus *is* the Christian life.

If Vocation is to mean anything, it means the wholehearted dedication of every faculty to the service of Jesus Christ – the use of opportunity to the full through the realization of it in every aspect – and the development of the entire person to the utmost, until, however novel the situation or strange the call, the servant of Christ will know instinctively what to do. Instinct in art and in life is not an accidental thing, or a gift which one has or has not – it is the outcome of experience and thought, so deep, so interwoven within the whole person, as to be sometimes hardly conscious, but always real and always intense. Christian instinct acts spontaneously and unconsciously, but it springs from a deliberate surrender to Christ and a deliberate, active, and intelligent association with him.

6

THE STATUE
OF THE GOOD SHEPHERD

IN the last chapter we took a backward step, so far as chronology is concerned. Here we move forward again, taking with us the idea involved in the parable of the Talents - that the person with a vocation must be prepared to know when to leave old paths and strike out new ones, perhaps without definite instructions that anyone would recognise, but acting on a Christian sense of situation.

To illustrate this I propose to turn to a forgotten sculptor who made a signal contribution to art. I have to confess at once that my reconstruction of this story is conjectural; but the elements of it, taken singly, are drawn from facts and experiences of which we have abundant contemporary evidence, and their combination simply involves imaginative shaping. It is possible that the story to be told is not true of the actual sculptor of whom we will have to think, but the story is true of the milieu in which the actual work of art was made. The story involves a piece of sculpture and, again, the authentic first example may have perished, but nonetheless, at or about the period with which we are dealing, some person had the conception which under his or her own hand and tool, or under the hand and tool of another commissioned by that person, took the form to which the type has ever since been true.

"A person of sense," said Plato in the *Phaedo*, speaking of one of his myths, "will not insist that these things are exactly as I've described them. But I think it will be believed that something of the kind is true." In the following story at least each detail given rests on actual records of Christian life about the end of the second century.

The man, then, was a sculptor – not of the great kind, no Michelangelo, but something like those people who today have their shops within a hundred yards of every large cemetery, who make conventional angels kneeling in prayer or hovering over a strong marble support, crosses, urns, and broken columns, and the like. He was rather the artisan than the artist – a man who worked from a pattern, and repeated it frequently.

This is not to say he had no ability for his work; like Lucian the satirist, he may have been put to work in an uncle's trade because he would scrape wax from the wax tablet that served as a slate for school and mould it into figures – but unlike Lucian who fled from the shop and his uncle's anger at a clumsy breakage, this man stuck to his trade.

He carved gods, like the statue sculptor presented in Aesop's fables who carves Jupiter and Juno, and the god

Mercury "with his rod and wings, and all the ensigns of his commission". When it comes to the price for the work Aesop's statue maker says, "Why truly, you seem to be a civil gentleman, give me but my price for the other two and you shall even have that other into the bargain."

Given the marble and the model, our sculptor can repeat the piece indefinitely, and much on the same level, each copy about as good as the one before it.

We may picture him living in a heathen town, a decent friendly kind of man, judged by the common standards, which would not exclude the ordinary pleasures of heathen mankind in what they would call moderation, but would hardly be "according to Christ" in Paul's phrase. Our sculptor came to know some Christian people, or some of his own friends turned Christian.

This amused him very much, and like other simple humorists of his own day, he welcomed the chance of a new object. He laughed at them and made a game at them, and they took it good-temperedly. Sometimes they argued sensibly with him, and then he grew flippant; sometimes they teased him back. There was plenty of ammunition in the lockers on both sides, and we know of some of the things actually said. "It's a poor heart that never rejoices," he said, "why do you never enjoy life, never wear even a garland?" They said they smelt with their noses, not their hair; and besides a crown of flowers was bad for the brain. On another day his cheery greeting was "Away with the Atheists!" – quoting one of the regular cries of the mob when it harried the Christians.

"Go into your shop," they said, "and ask the spiders what they think of your gods." Or sometimes he would warn them they would yet stand at the pro-consul's tribunal, if they did not take care; and they would reply gravely that they must all be manifested at the tribunal of Christ.

So things went on. He made fun of them, but he was not unfriendly. Then they asked him straight out: "Why not come to our meeting and see for yourself what we do and what we teach?" He hung back for a while, and they had a handle on him now – how much easier it was to judge when you didn't know!

At last he went, and then he went a number of times. It was all very simple, and absurd and improbable; but he grew interested – in the story of Christ in Galilee, appearing in that strange and humiliating form; in the stories He told, in the parables and teaching of God's love. It was absurd, of course; and one day, perhaps he picked up the parody of it that Celsus had in his book: how the frogs sat around in their pond, and croaked a story of God becoming one of them because he loved them, and meant to save the frogs who believed – and even the tadpoles – when He burned the rest of the world with fire, like a clumsy cook.

All the same, our sculptor began to see there was something in the lives of these people that answered to their faith, and he became impressed with their story of the death of Jesus, as men and women always are when they come to it in any real way – so like the death of Socrates, and so different in shame and betrayal. Of course the Resurrection was just a tale, and the Last Judgement a myth, but an uncomfortable myth.

One day he went to the amphitheatre. It was one of his pleasures, and he took care to get a good place, wedged in amongst the shouting crowd. Today here was great excitement, and it was soon clear there was to be some trouble about the Christians. He grew uncomfortable, but he could not get out – besides, it might have looked suspicious. Perhaps the spies who had denounced them might recognise him – what a fool he had been! Then came a great shout, and he looked up and saw his Christian friends in the arena, stripped naked and tied to stakes; and the whole amphitheatre howling derision and hatred at them – shouting for the beasts. Did his friends see him? Did they suspect he was the traitor? The hideous scene dragged on – each moment an age – then the lions; and what they left the soldiers cut the throats of. It is all in the *Acts of the Martyrdom of Felicitas and Perpetua*, and we need not linger over it.

The man went home, tingled and disturbed. Some days of work in his shop followed – days of thought and feeling and upheaval. On the Sunday night he sought out what was left of the Christian group. They eyed him curiously at first. But he explained why he had come, and asked for baptism. They were in no hurry to give it; they let him wait, to learn as a catechumen; and at last, when Easter day came, clad in white he was baptized, renouncing in so many words "the devil and his pomp and his angels." They sealed him and gave him the symbol or creed, and he was conscious by-and-by of a new experience – the Holy Spirit, they said.

Whether all this happened to our sculptor or not, it did to other men; Tertullian himself, I think, among them – from his pages come much set out here.

The sculptor went back to his shop – living a new life, full of new feelings, and meeting the ups and downs all Christians know. He went on with his trade, until one Sunday a man at the meeting spoke of idolatry, and picked out one profession and another tainted with it, and, drawing his bow at a venture cried, "You are a sculptor. How have you renounced the devil and his pomps and his angels, you who make your living by them? But you say, A man must live! *Must* he? There are no *musts* with God. Still, it is commonly done! Jesus Christ our Lord called Himself truth, not custom."

It was not only sculptors and painters and the like that came under scrutiny; the teachers of the Classics were included – idolaters all in fact, whatever they said they believed – and above all was the tribunal of Christ.

Our sculptor went home in trouble. It *was* true. He had been living off the devil and his angels, carving their images. With a sigh, he turned the statues to face the wall – he was done with them for good. He could at least be a stone mason, which the classical teacher could not. So to the stones he went, and squared them – square stones, flat stones, flat stones and square stones, and eternal monotony of right angles and flat surfaces – never the shoulders of Venus or the head of Apollo rising from the block with their curves. No more curves – at best, poor pomegranates and endless garlands, but never the free glad touch of his art! What a life – and yet it was for Christ that he made this sacrifice.

At last the thought came to him – why not a statue of Christ himself? It had not been done, and there was no model, and he was not good original designs. Christians had used little devices in the flat – e.g. a fish to represent Christ, in virtue of the fish's Greek name, making an acrostic of "Jesus Christ, God's Son Saviour." But he wanted something more.

Finally, one Sunday, someone spoke on the parable of the Lost Sheep, and the sculptor saw Jesus the Good Shepherd carrying the sheep home – and he also saw a heathen god, Hermes the Ram-bearer. He had not thought of that before. This time he went home in gladness, and he set about the statue of the Good Shepherd – he had his inspiration, and how good the tools felt in his hand!

His Good Shepherd bore a strong likeness to Hermes the Ram-bearer; and it was not a very good piece of work – stiff and conventional, artisan work as ever – but it told a tale. It was not Hermes, it was Christ; and in his rough stone he had embodied three great things. The Good Shepherd stood there with the sheep, found and on His shoulders – and as the sculptor looked at it he could almost fancy the joy in the presence of the angels. In the next place, he had worked into his stone the gist of the

Christian Gospel – that God had sent the Good Shepherd, and that He is always seeking the lost, until He find them. And in the third place – and here he had to meet critics, who told him he had confused the Good Shepherd in John's Gospel with the everyday ordinary shepherd of the parable in Luke's Gospel, because the Good Shepherd in the gospel of John never carried a sheep. "Didn't he?" said the sculptor, "Well, you see, I wanted to have my own story in it, too." And so he had.

It was true that he had mixed up the parables, that he had made Christ surprisingly like a Greek god – one of the devil's angels – and that he had a most pagan zest in handling the old tools, until he had begun to wonder if his motives were as pure as he thought; but he had given art a great type for all that, for he had worked from his heart and wrought a Christian's experience of his saviour into stone. And every new such translation of it is a new Gospel. He had renounced what he loved best in the world for Christ; and in Christ he had found all again – the lost art, the lost curves, the lost joy of creative work – and he had given the Christian Church a new voice, a new and eternal expression of the central truth of the Gospel.

His name has gone; in all probability the very stone he carved has gone; but the work remains, and the type he gave stands for ever one of the two great symbols that tell men and women of Christ.

APPENDIX I

The Meaning of Christmas Day

T R Glover

Essay in *The Pilgrim*
SCM Press, 1921

EVERYBODY knows what Christmas Day is. We know it so well that we do not think about it. But it often repays us to think about the things that we know best and, without embarking on theology, we may say that Christmas Day commemorates the birth of the most interesting man known to history.

We can admit at once that we have no means of knowing when he really was born. It was not till the middle of the fourth century that December 25th was chosen to commemorate the birth of Jesus Christ. The day had its own associations; it was a Roman festival time when, for a few days, all slaves were free and their own masters. It was also kept, over a large part of the world, as "The Day of the Unconquered Sun." There was a widespread worship of the Sun and, after the shortest day of the year and the dark days round about it, the growth of the Sun's light is evident on December 25th, and the day was kept as the birthday of the Sun. Not a bad day after all on which to remember the birth of Jesus, a day associated with freedom, the day that celebrates the birth of light.

This man's birth has meant both freedom and light to humans, and it is worthwhile to let our minds rest on what he has done, on what he has meant to men and women.

Jesus stands for the God-centred life. There never was anyone for whom God was so real, for whom God was so near, and this sense of his for God lies at the very heart of all that he has done in bringing men and women freedom and light. It was not that he did not know the darkness and the limitations of ordinary life. As we read his story we can see that his was no easy life. If he believed in God it was not for want of knowledge of hell. He lived in a land enslaved by foreigners; he was a carpenter, he was poor. One of the early Fathers of the Church reminded the Christian rich that the Lord Jesus brought no silver footbath from heaven. He had to work for a widowed mother, for little brothers and sisters; he knew the tragedy of the money being lost, and the joy when it was found. He knew how hard it is to keep children in food and clothes, how fast they wear their clothes out, and how the time comes when clothes can be patched no more. He lived in a little town which, like other little towns, had its stories of squalor and pain, of broken lives, of prodigal sons, of oppression and tyranny. We can see in his story that he knew our problems, that he knew above all where they hurt. " He suffered," we read in the New Testament, and it tells us what he did suffer — conflict of mind, temptation, repudiation, betrayal. The story is summed up as agony. All these things he knew, the commonplace troubles of ordinary people, the soul-destroying tragedies that from time to time break down the best and most beautiful spirits. He knew life, and he had the intellectual habit of taking the incidents of life without an anaesthetic, the hero's way of facing what is to be borne with open eyes and unflinching.

This man brings home to us, both by his teaching and by the story of his life, the possibility of real contact with God, not in mere moments of exaltation, but in the steady, sober business of life, in its enjoyments, in its sorrows, and in the happiness which we take without noticing. For him the centre of every thing is God. God is not for him a vague abstract noun; he never defines God as if God were a problem in philosophy. But he lives on the basis of God, in the presence of God; he accepts God as a child accepts the best sort of father; God is there, God is good, and kind, and fatherly, and a friend, and a lover, One Who shares all our interests, Who never excludes anything in our lives from His mind or from His heart. Children always know when their parents are really interested in their affairs; the dolls, the stamp collection, the little house among the bushes, the bow and arrow. The great thing that Jesus gives us is this conviction that God is interested in us, down to the last details of everything that appeals to our own minds and natures, and that He is interested in us because He is fond of us. For example, if you have not thought about these things, track down through the Gospels the references of Jesus to God's interest in colours. Jesus speaks of God's interest in the lily, which, he says, for beauty beats "Solomon in all his glory." It is quite clear that colour, and movement, and form, all the things that make the life of nature, appealed to Jesus, and he saw that they all appeal to God. Other teachers had taught people to use the ingenuity of the universe as an argument for the existence of a Mind behind it. Jesus was touched by the beauty of living things, and he saw that their beauty means that God, like every other creative mind, loves beauty. In this way Jesus brings God near to us ; God, Who really likes and enjoys flowers and sparrows, would probably like little children, and Jesus says that He does.

It is not only that Jesus sees what a delightful nature God really has, but he is able to translate it into life. His knowledge of God is not like our knowledge of some things which we use when we want them (if we ever use them at all), but it is translated into life with this result, that it gives life a new worth-while-ness. His own life, his own personality, guarantee his insight into God. What is more, is the power he has of winning people to his outlook, of launching them on the new kind of life that he lived, and (seeing we are using a metaphor from ships) of steering them when they are launched, and safeguarding them from all the submarine activities of the enemy of life. That he does this still, is the experience of Christians.

Let us look a little at what his coming has meant in human history. Nothing has been more effective in safeguarding the individual man and woman from wrong and oppression than the conviction that he, or she, was one for whom Christ died. If Christ died for the slave, then we must at least be kind to him, and one day we shall set him free. If Christ died for the prostitute, then we shall have to re-think the conduct of life, and our whole estimate of women. There can be no exploiting people for whom Christ died. (This, by the way, is the essence of sin, the exploitation of people and the using of God's gifts against God.) Historically, where men and women have believed that Christ died for the least important of us, there has been a new honour for men and women, a new love for them, and a growing resolve that everything shall be theirs which their Great Friend could wish them to have. In this way Jesus has been the best champion of the people. Jesus increases the significance of humans for one another; "he possessed and he conveys the genius for appreciation." The definition of a gentleman as "one who does not put his feeling before others' rights, or his rights before their feelings" is exactly in the vein of Jesus. There may be those who see little in courtesy and good manners, but Jesus saw their inner meaning, and he taught and practised them. They are a recognition of the dignity of God's children. There was a charm about his love that he has been able to transmit to many of his followers. Charm is an unconscious thing, and it is never really acquired by practice, but Jesus taught his followers to forget themselves, and many of them have learnt the lesson, and catching his spirit have caught a great deal of his charm.

Jesus was the great discoverer of the family. We are so familiar with the text, "Suffer little children to come unto me", that we forget what a new and original thing it was for a great man and a great teacher to say. He believed in family life; he never taught that all the best men and women should not marry, he held with their marrying; and biologists today emphasize the boundless spiritual and intellectual gain to society, when, at the Reformation, marriage was given the significance that Jesus saw it has in God's scheme of things. It is pointed out how much the world owes to the good men and women who have married and brought up children. This is part of the freedom that Jesus has given us, and this, too, must be linked with his consciousness of God.

The 16th century saw the New Testament translated into English, the story of Jesus made available "for the boy that follows the plough"; and the 17th century saw a great revolution in England, a great achievement of freedom. The 18th century saw the great campaign of the Wesleys to win men and women for Jesus Christ; the 19th century saw England abolish the slave trade, humanize laws, emancipate women. Why is it that where Jesus becomes a living reality for men and women, they are more human than before, larger of soul and of sympathy?

For a long time before Jesus was born, people had been wrestling with the idea that even foreigners are human. Jesus himself is the great pledge that we all are of one blood, "barbarian, Scythian, bond and free," English, German, Indian and Chinese. There is a certain truth in nationalism, but Jesus made humanity a real thing in God. He must lay the foundations for any League of Nations that is to be real and to last.

For the individual, Jesus has done wonderful things. His very existence has historically been a stimulus to thought. We forget sometimes that thought is a primary Christian duty. We forget the freedom of mind of Jesus, and his perpetual insistence on our thinking. "The truth shall make you free," we read; but the truth is not found at random, in the streets. Jesus has committed us to finding out and incorporating in life all the truth there is in God, to capturing the whole of God, and making God in all His fullness our own. He has not only set men and women this task, but he helps them to achieve it. Very much the same can be said about art as about the other regions of thought and feeling. One function of art is the enjoyment and the interpretation of "God's realm" in its whole complex of relations. Was there ever anyone who enjoyed God more than Jesus did? or shared his joy in God more successfully with other people, communicating his joy to men and women? Jesus was more than what we call original, he was originative; he had the creative mind. His parables are masterpieces in the use of language, so easy and so simple that one would not suppose there was any art in them. That is the very acme of art. Jesus gave to the individual an infinite value, and by doing so he opened new fields to art. Wherever the story of Jesus has ruled, with its freedom and with its breadth, people have loved art and music and laughter, and have enjoyed all the simple and wonderful things that God gives. Humour has been defined as the sense of contrast touched by love, the power of seeing the finite on the background of the infinite. "The real sense of humour breaks into flower when we have overcome the world." Yes, and who overcomes the world? Who has the real peace of mind that is essential to humour but those whom Jesus has made free of the whole world, by showing them that they are the children of God, and that the world is the home God has made for them, and by giving them the courage to see God and to enjoy Him?

Jesus has enlarged the capacity of men and women for God; he has made us feel that the Author of every aspect of life touches the human spirit at every point. He has made us free, to develop our characters to the utmost; we are to be perfect as God is perfect. That includes every kind of perfection, intellectual and artistic, as well as moral and spiritual. Jesus has made God intelligible to us. He has brought God into our business and bosom, and he has given us the sense and the appetite for God. He has made us at home in God, and above all he has given us the feeling that the great joy of life is to realize God in every fibre of one's being, and to explore God through all the infinite maze of wonder and of love in which He shows Himself. Jesus has lit up God for us, turned light upon Him, and shown us that the great power of which we are afraid is the best Friend we have. In ancient days, and in the heathen world today, the object of religion is to get away from God. Jesus has changed all that, and made the object of our religion to get into the heart of God. He has interpreted God to us, for he himself is the bond of kinship between us. He is the author of peace, the giver of a happy mind, and that is why, to this day, we keep Christmas. Christmas is the Children's Day; what better day is there for them to keep than the birthday of the Great Friend, who (as it were) discovered them, who liked them, and was fonder of them than any of the world's great teachers, and who taught us all to love children with a new tenderness, and a new interest that the world had never known before?

So the ancient Church perhaps did not make a bad choice, when it chose the day associated with freedom and light, with the rebirth of nature, on which to remember the coming of Jesus. We shall use the day to the best purpose if we set our minds to work to discover, this Christmas, some new features of the Jesus whom we commemorate, if we read the Gospels over again and find out for ourselves what Jesus was and what he is. It is not a day on which we are called to celebrate a dead Jesus, but one which speaks to us of life, and calls us to come face to face with a Friend, who is waiting to talk with us, to help us, to set us free, and to give us the light we need to face the darkness round about us.

APPENDIX II

Jesus in the Experience of Men

T R Glover

Review by Revd Dr Howard Worsley, Vice-Principal, Trinity Theological College, Bristol

This book by Baptist scholar Terrot Glover (1869-1943) was published during his time as Public Orator at Cambridge University, where he lectured on classical literature (1920-1939). *Jesus in the Experience of Men* echoes the theme of a similar and better known book, *The Jesus of History* published a year later. These books show Glover's historical awareness as he draws on rich classical knowledge that is also informed by wider reading into psychological theory that was contemporary at the time of writing.

In the introduction to *Jesus in the Experience of Men* Glover writes, 'Our task is primarily historical' (xv) and he sets out to explore who Jesus is perceived to be from the lens of ancient history as understood by the Greeks, the early Church and later Church history. Glover attempts to explore the religious concepts of sin, forgiveness, salvation and justice within the experience of humans and as recorded throughout history. He looks at how the Church has wrestled with its own existence in relation to understanding Jesus and he goes further in considering the impact of the ideas of Jesus upon human progress and the human spirit. As he writes, Glover takes the role of an historian who is inviting the reader to be a theologian who reflects and analyses his insights.

The book is written with an awareness of what was then 'modern psychology', clearly drawing on Freud's understanding of the unconscious that had become widely accepted in his lifetime. Glover's particular strength is in drawing attention to ancient Jewish epistemological thought, noting for example the prevalence of demonology within Pauline thinking that is then generally subsequently abandoned within Christian discourse. This discussion has since been greatly developed via the writings of Walter Winks whose seminal books on The Powers, *Naming the Powers* (1984), *Unmasking the Powers* (1986), *Engaging the Powers* (1992), *When the Powers Fall* (1998) and *The Powers that Be* (1999) all lead him to an understanding of non-violent resistance.

Similarly Glover's handling of the Christian problem of divine justice details how all things are perceived to lead towards a final reckoning in which a saviour is required to atone. In this he boldly considers the underlying philosophical constructs that have influenced Jewish, Platonic and Christian thought. In the fourth chapter, entitled 'The Lamb of God', he has a particularly clear means of overviewing what we might now call 'models of atonement'. Since the 1920s, such study has been developed in terms of how atonement is perceived, as is seen in the writings of Gerard (*Violence and the Sacred*, 1972) whose concept of 'mimetic desire' has developed engagement between psychological and theological disciplines.

Throughout the book we see the author's clear mind offering succinct and orderly thinking of how Jesus has become understood as Saviour and Lord. It is a mind that is committed to following Jesus whilst also unpicking how the detail of such revelation has been understood and accepted by the Church over time.

Glover's conclusion is that Jesus 'has enlarged Man's capacity for God and has satisfied it.' He writes,

> Jesus all through the centuries has been making the human heart larger, and more human, and more apt to get hold of God and then to want more of him…Where the spirit of the Lord Jesus is, there is liberty. (p 258)

This is a book that needs to be re-read in current times when progression in human thought seems to be wilting as a concept within theological or philosophical thinking. *Jesus in the Experience of Men* is a welcome reminder of an era when theology drew confidently from the insights of other disciplines. Currently, theology seems to be in danger of becoming stale with voices purporting generous orthodoxy whilst simultaneously narrowing theological breadth, and other voices suggesting a radical orthodoxy whilst disavowing the insights of modernity. Reading Glover is a refreshing reminder of an earlier period, only a century ago, that was charged with the hope of human progression in thought, and this makes it both insightful, hopeful and stimulating.

Howard Worsley
Wells, May 2020

INDEX

79

Also available from Beauchief Abbey Press:

T R Glover

The Jesus of History

With a modern introduction by

J W Rogerson

www.beauchiefabbeypress.org